THIS NOTEBOOK BELONGS TO

....

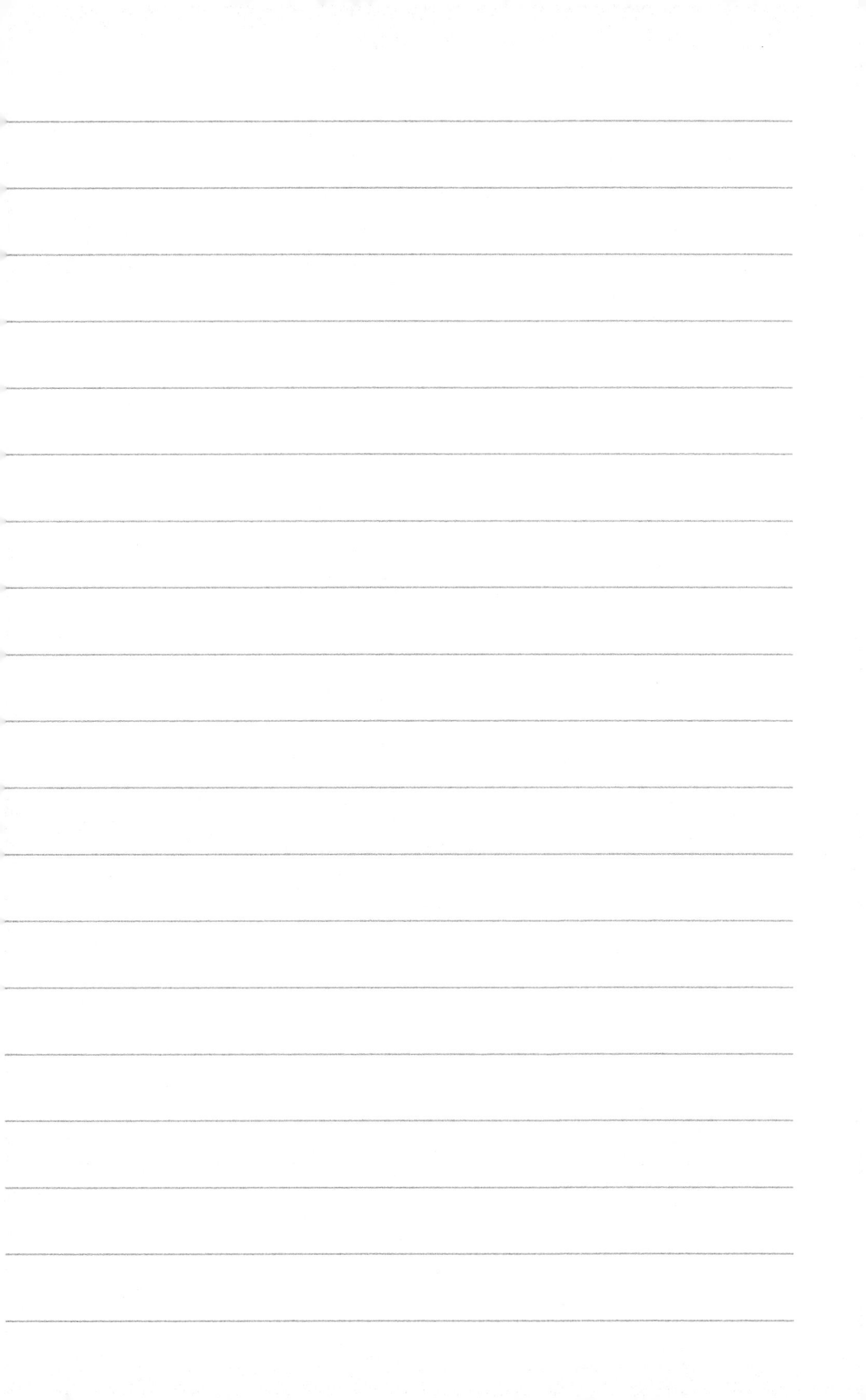

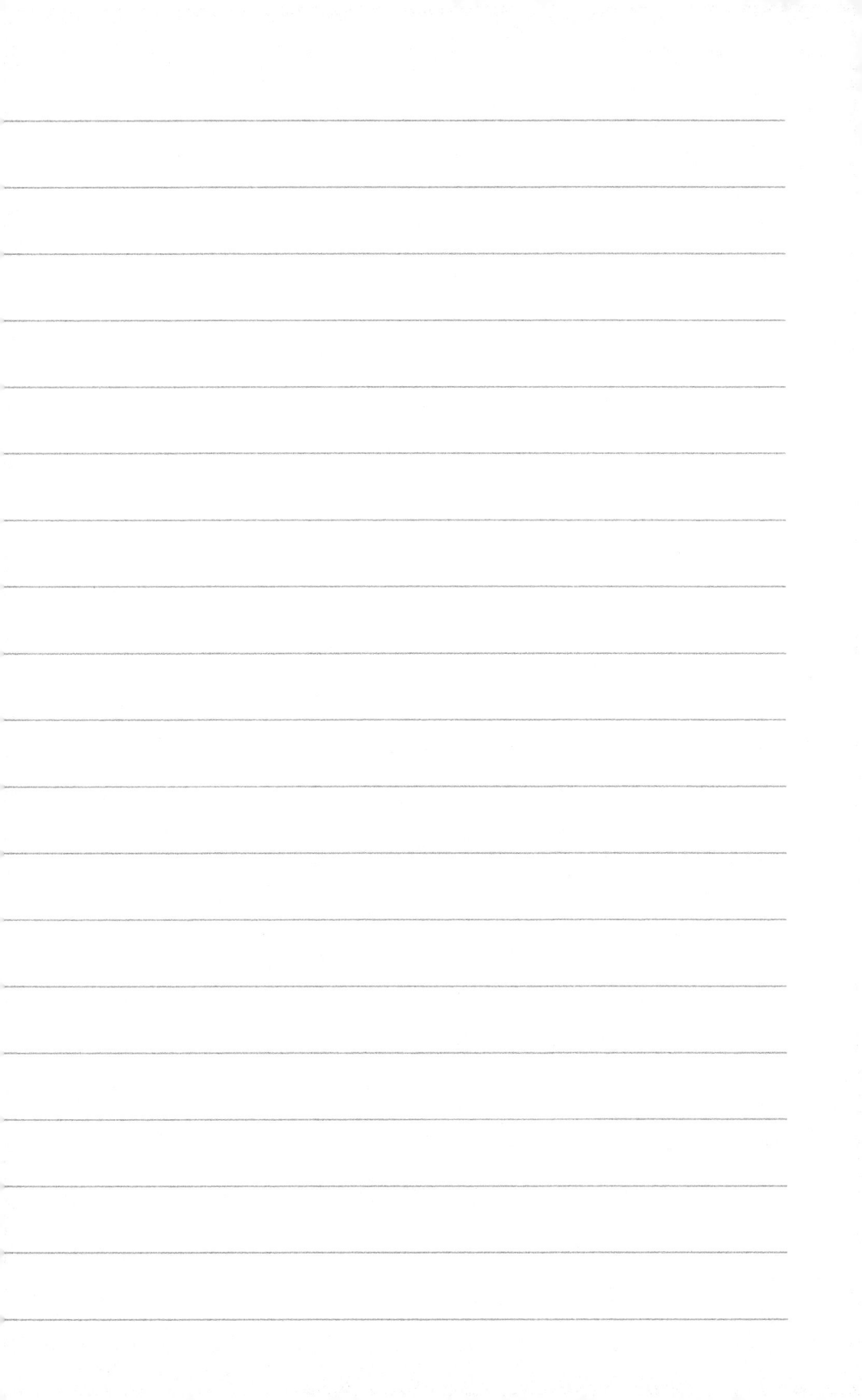

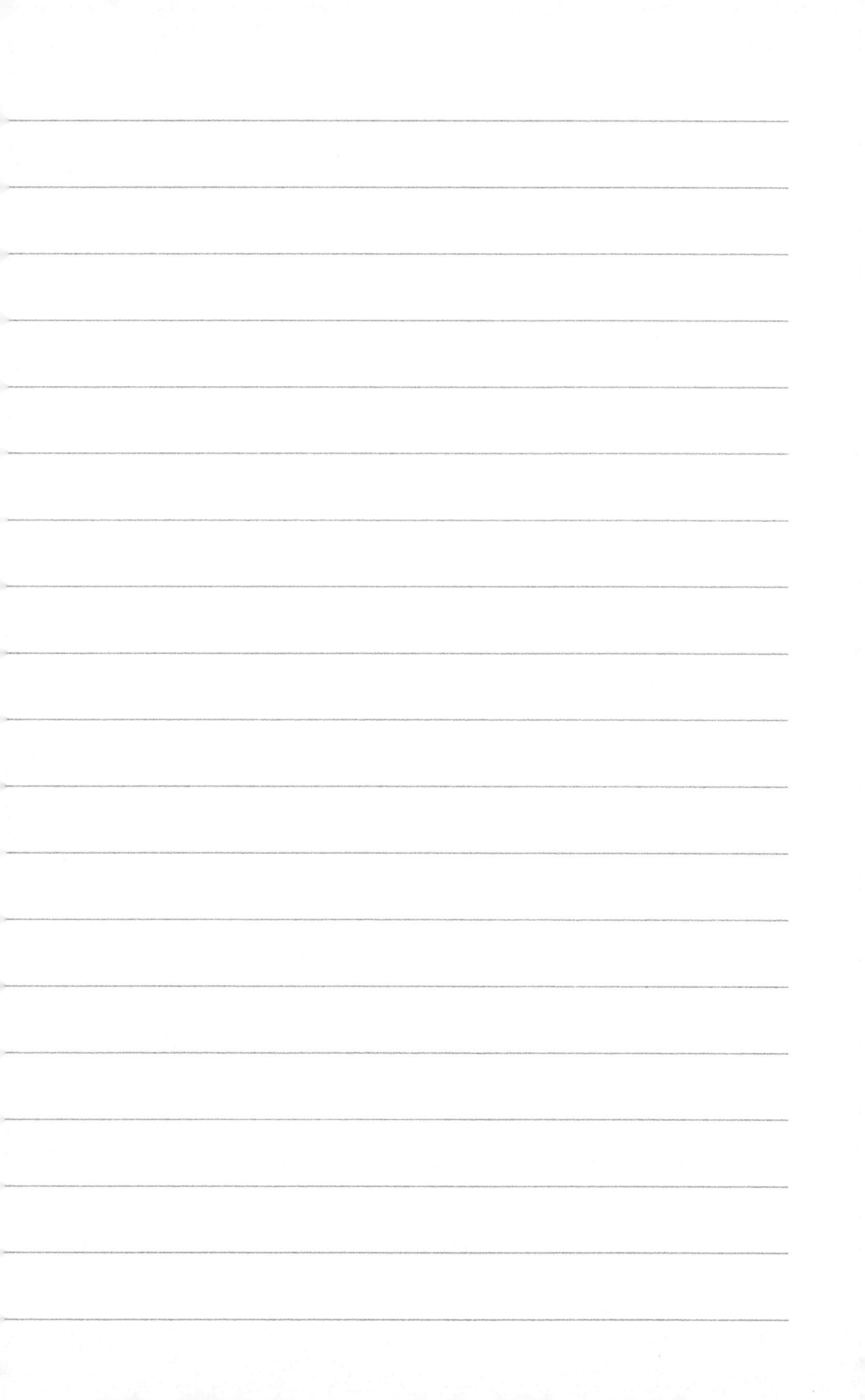

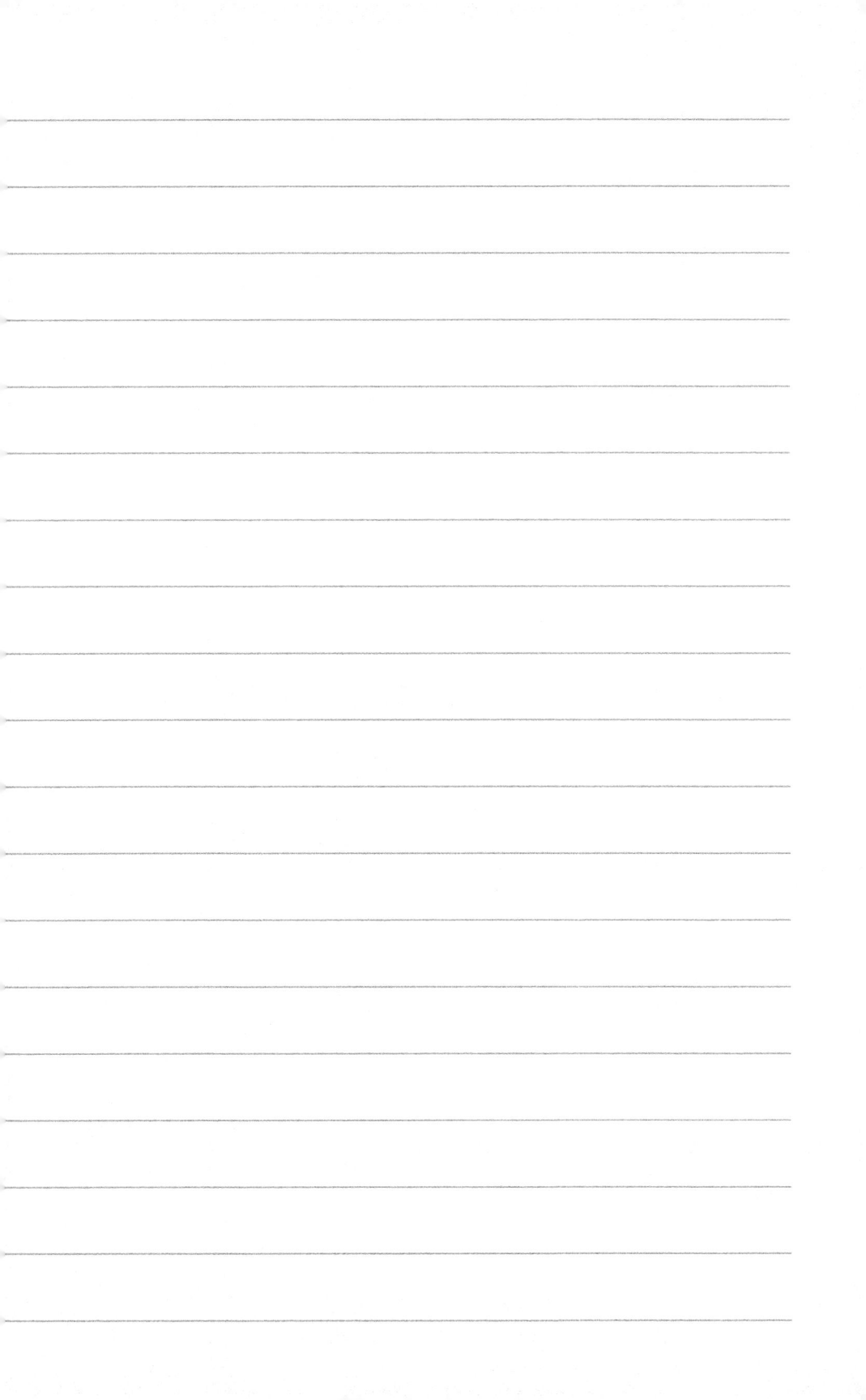

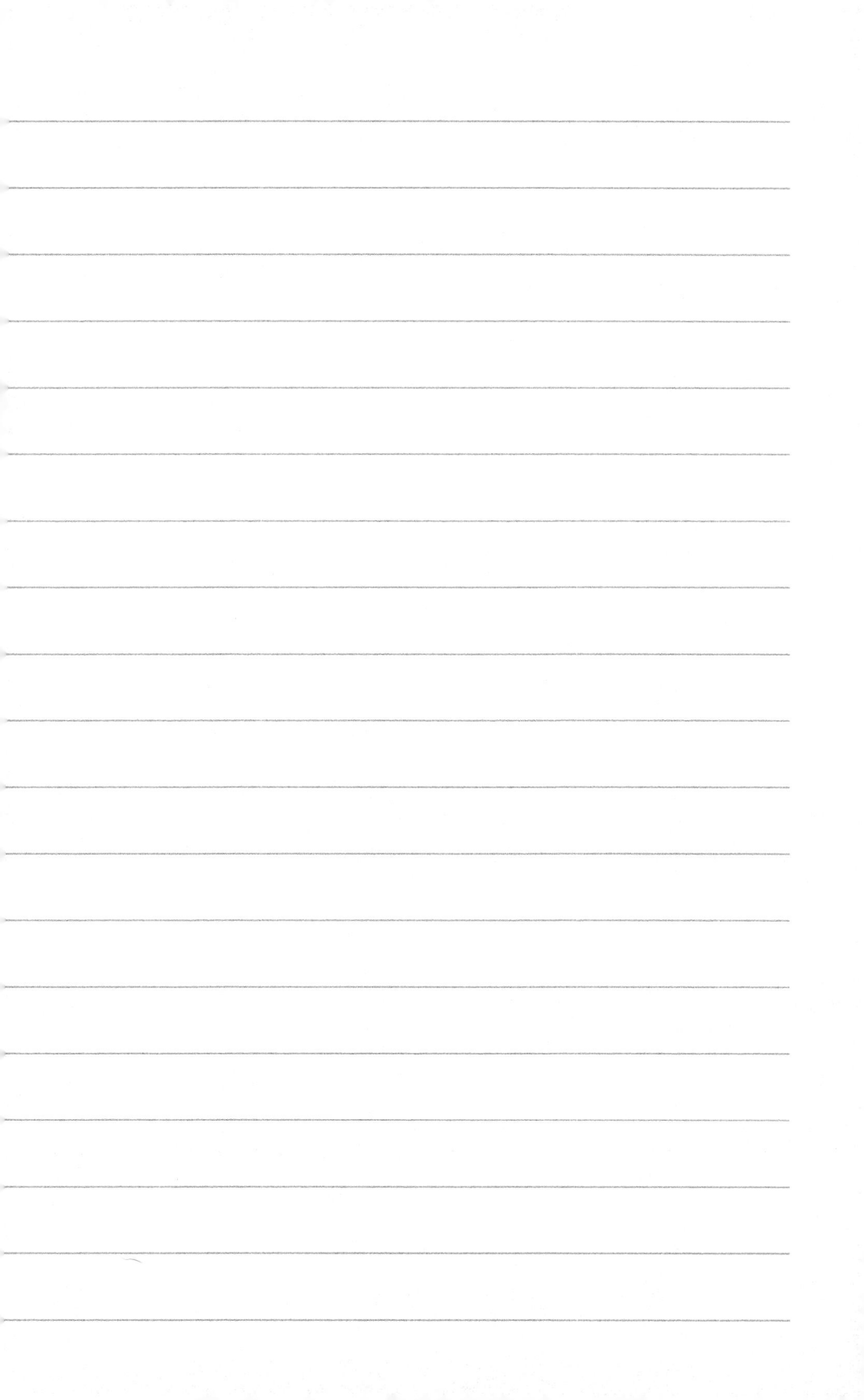

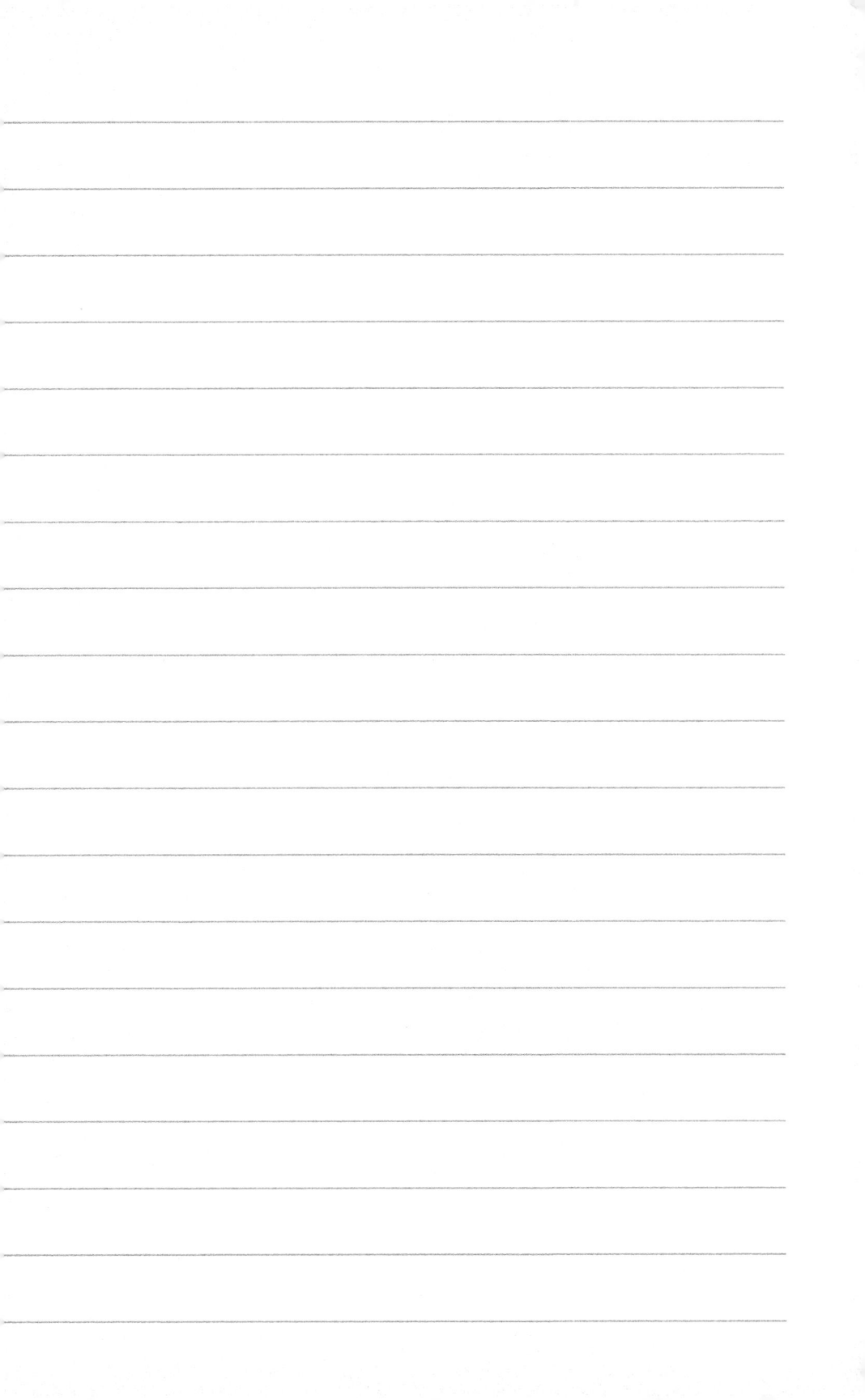

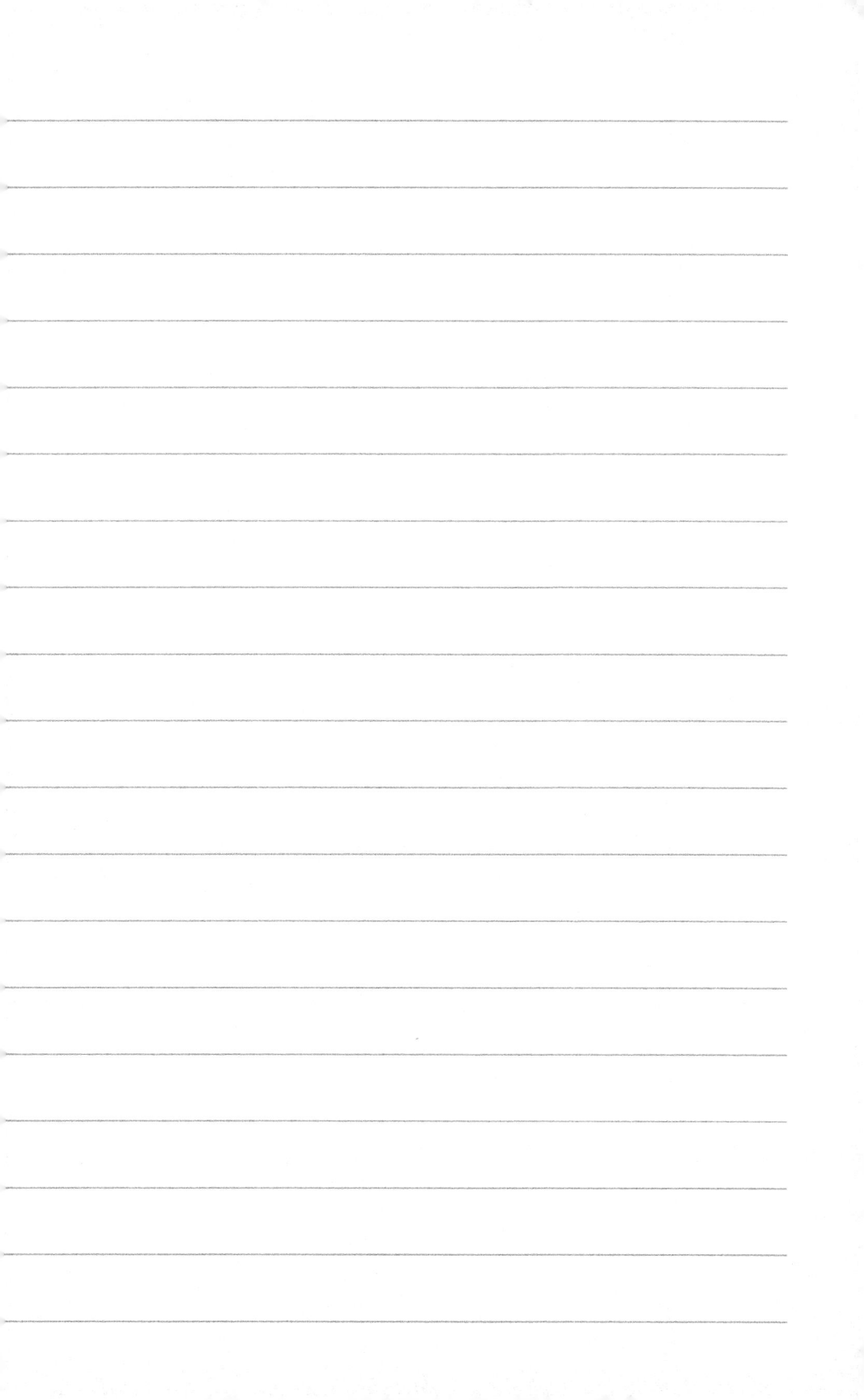

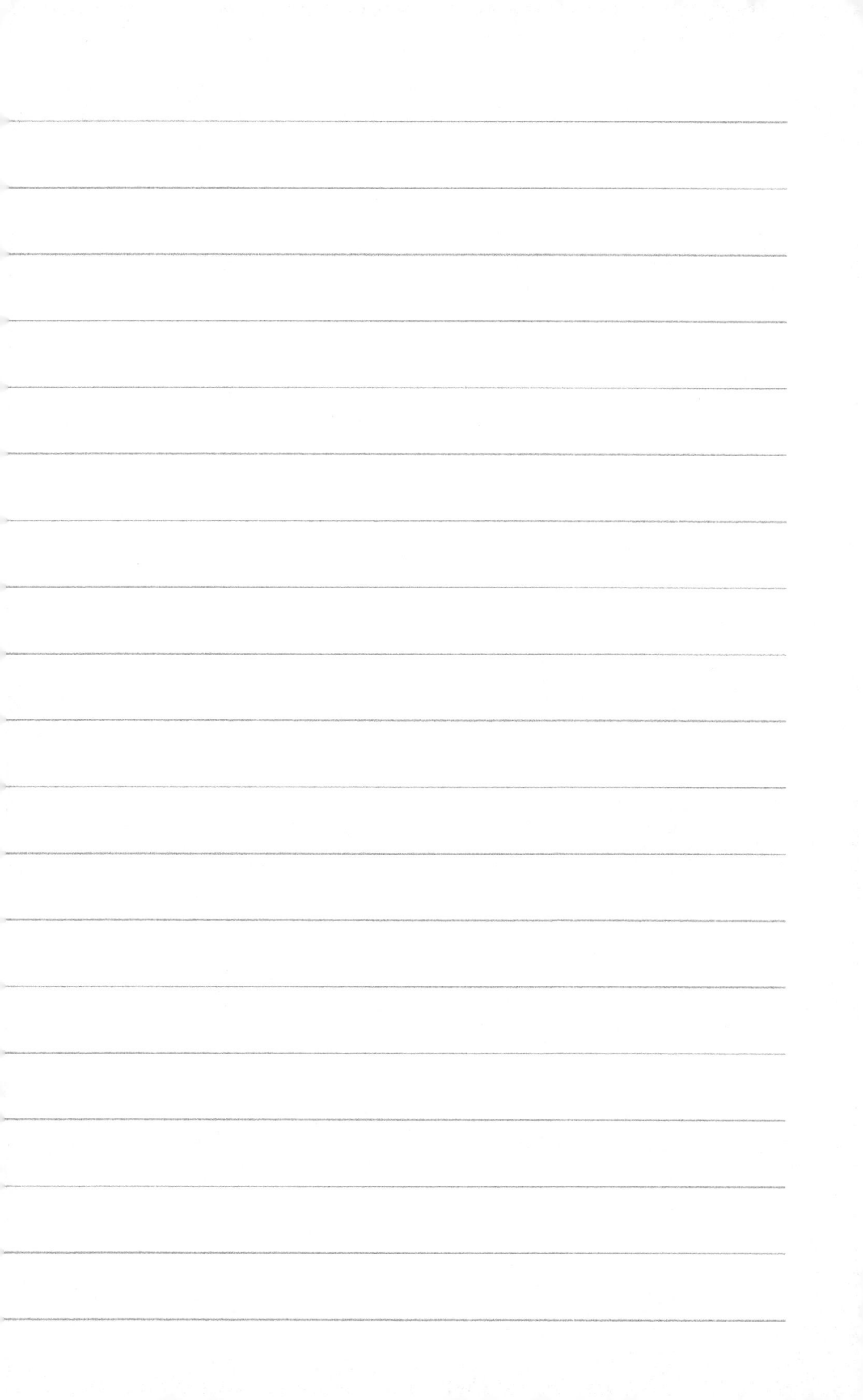

Made in the USA
Las Vegas, NV
16 December 2023

82968094R00069